PROSPERITY IS GOD'S IDEA

Margaret M. Stevens

Illustrations by David Stevens

DeVORSS & CO., *Publishers*
P.O. Box 550
Marina del Rey, CA 90294–0550

Third Printing 1987

ISBN: 0-87516-264-9

Printed in the United States of America

I wish to acknowledge and thank all who have helped me to understand and practice the principles set forth in this book.

Particularly do I want to express my deep gratitude to two special people . . .

Dr. Raymond N. Holliwell, for his inspiration and encouragement, and for starting me off on the road to prosperous living,

and

my husband, Roger, for being such an understanding, supportive, and loving companion as we travel together on this exciting adventure.

Many thanks to Dr. William Goldmann, whose valuable suggestions helped to make this book possible.

TABLE OF CONTENTS

INTRODUCTION

If you have struggled, perhaps for years, trying to make your available money cover all your needs . . .

If you have felt cheated out of life's blessings . . .

If you have envied another's possessions or life-style . . .

If you think that poverty and limitation are God's idea, and that you might as well get used to living without the luxuries and comforts of abundant living . . .

READ ON!!!
THIS BOOK WAS WRITTEN FOR YOU

By way of brief introduction, let me say that I have experienced all these feelings, and it was a red-letter day in my life when I first heard the words, "God loves a prosperous person," spoken by one of our greatest New Thought leaders many years ago. This was a revelation for one who was brought up to think that it is a Christian virtue to be poor and taught to expect the reward for such virtue in heaven. Then along came a successful man who

1

said, "God wants you to be successful. God is not honored or glorified or praised when He sees human beings crawling around in poverty. You are made in the image and likeness of God. God is in the business of distributing His limitless wealth to people who will think big." Jesus said, "I am come that you might have life and have it abundantly."

PROSPERITY . . . WHAT IS IT?

Prosperity means different things to different people . . . to you it may mean lots of money, or freedom to do what you want to do. To someone else it might be the difference between starvation and having enough to eat. For others, prosperity could mean the ability and the means to enjoy the luxuries of life. The best definition of prosperity that I have found is this: *The ability to do what you want to do when you want to do it.* If, at this moment, you want a cup of coffee and a hamburger, and you have the money to purchase them, you are prosperous.

Prosperity does not just mean having enough money. True prosperity includes an abundance of all the good things in life . . . good health, right relationships, satisfying work AND a more than ample supply of money.

Prosperity is really a state of mind . . . a feeling. In the days before I discovered the real meaning of prosperity, I could capture the feeling of being prosperous just by going to the nearest drug store to purchase a new lipstick!

Money is a symbol of God's opulence, beauty and abundance. It is a symbol of economic health in an individual or a nation. When your blood is circulating freely, you are healthy. When money is circulating freely in your life, you are economically healthy. When you begin to hoard, when you refuse to spend for fear there won't be enough to go around, there is economic illness.

The stock market crash of 1929 was a perfect example of this kind of panic as a sort of hypnotic spell fell over millions of people (How wonderful if the reverse should happen!). Can't you just imagine millions of people suddenly alive with new optimism and hope, understanding the laws of prosperity and spending and using their money freely and wisely?

You can live in absolute freedom, living by spiritual principle, knowing that in spite of depressions, strikes, wars, you will always be amply supplied, regardless of change in the form of exchange. You can depend on the fact that like the tide that goes out, and always comes back in, your supply may go out, but it will always come back to you because you are depending on a tireless, changeless, immortal presence of good, God.

Know that God's opulence is for you, whether you have earned it or not—it is God's love in action.

Prosperity really *is* God's idea, and Christianity teaches a wonderful concept about money. In fact, Jesus talked more about money or supply than any other subject, so He must have realized its importance. The truth is that prosperity has its basis in spiritual law. Moses said to the Hebrew people, "You shall remember the Lord your God, for it is He who gives you power to get wealth."

In this statement we find the whole secret of supply. God is the only source of all that is. Not only is God the source, but He is the supply itself. Jobs and investments and people and connections are simply the channels of that supply, but always God is the source. This is why you need not panic or even be disturbed if you lose your job, or if some investment fails. When you understand the infallible principle behind the demonstration of supply, you will know that one channel is closing so that God can open a new and better one for you.

Let's look at some of the familiar Bible quotations concerning supply:

I am the Lord thy God which teacheth thee to profit, which leadeth thee by the way thou shouldst go.

Isaiah 48:17

They shall prosper that love Thee.

Psalm 122

Eye hath not seen nor ear heard, neither have entered into the heart of man the things which God hath prepared for them that love Him.

1st Corinthians 2:9

They that seek the Lord shall not want any good thing.

Psalm 34:10

There is no doubt that all people experience ups and downs which seem to be inevitable in life, but once you get in touch with this marvelous principle, seeing God as the source and the supply, prosperity is assured.

Beloved, I wish above all things that thou mayest prosper and be in health, even as thy soul prospers.

The word "beloved" is usually reserved for those for whom we have a strong affection, and in this verse we are being spoken to as a much-loved offspring of God.

Many people who are materially wealthy are in great poverty when it comes to friendship, or inner peace of mind. Others have everything except money. You are prosperous to the degree that you are experiencing health, peace and abundance in your life. You can have all of this world's goods that you could possibly want, but if you are troubled in mind, if you are constantly worried about something, you are not truly prosperous. Remember that money is a spiritual idea and the more you have circulating in your life (not hoarded), the more you are expressing God, which is your real reason for being.

I have known people to experience miracles in their lives through the use of a powerful affirmation, based on this verse:

I am a beloved child of God and He wants me to prosper and be in health.

Not only is it all right for you to prosper, but if you don't, you are not living up to God's will, which is always for your highest good. Living in want and limitation is denying God the full expression of His life through you. "Poverty is a mental disease and should be abolished from the face of the earth," said Ernest Holmes.

Now what about some misconceptions that keep people from living prosperous, free lives? Have you ever thought that prosperity depends on luck? That's one idea you must discard at once. This is a universe of law and order. There are dependable laws that operate regardless of what we think of them, or whether we even know about them. We do certain things and there are corresponding results. Your prosperity depends upon your willingness to accept the Truth and let it operate in your life.

Have you ever wondered why so many good people lead impoverished lives? Remember that the law of belief works regardless of how good or how evil one is. If you believe your lot to be one of poverty, it will be, regardless of how "good" you may be. On the other hand, it seems as if the wicked of the world often enjoy life's greatest benefits, and it just doesn't seem fair. But again, remember that we are dealing with a principle which says, "As you think in your heart, so are you." It doesn't say, "As you wish, or desire," but "As you think in your heart" (the deep feeling part of you). If your attitude is one of fear and anxiety about your life, you will attract conditions conforming to that belief.

Do you see money as evil? That one verse in Paul's letter to Timothy has caused more heartache and suffering than almost any other passage in the Bible. Paul said,

"The love of money is the root of all evil." The money isn't evil, but an inordinate love of it can be wrong. Love of money to the exclusion of everything else, giving it first place in your life, will cause you to become unbalanced and out of harmony with the flow of life. The evil comes from man's darkened understanding, from his false interpretation of life and his misuse of the Divine power.

You are here to use your power and authority wisely. If you see prosperity as money only, you do not understand the matter of supply. Nature insists on a balance. If all your time is devoted to the gathering of material things and possessions, you may find yourself hungry for peace of mind, love, joy or health. You will find that you cannot buy anything that is real or lasting. "Seek ye first the kingdom of heaven [the consciousness of all-good] and all these things [the material possessions] will be added."

Have you ever felt that you are unworthy? Remember that you are a child of God and therefore you inherit His bounty in the form of every good thing.

A woman stood at the long check-out line in the supermarket late one afternoon. Her pretty face was lined with fatigue marks and her whole body drooped. The woman behind her in the line watched for a few moments, then she spoke softly to the younger woman, whom we will call Jane. "Are you feeling all right, dear? You look so tired and pale." Jane turned around wearily, and answered in an almost inaudible voice, "No, I'm not all right. I'm exhausted from a frightful day at the office. Now I have to buy groceries, hurry home, fix dinner, wash some clothes and get the children to bed. Then tomorrow morning I have to be up at five o'clock, fix breakfast, lunches,

9

and hurry for the bus. It's the same dismal routine day after day, and I can't see any end in sight." The older woman began to talk quietly, but boldly. She said, "I used to feel almost the same way; then I discovered how wonderful life can be when one comes to see himself as a child of God, with a loving Father who really cares." Jane was in no mood to hear a sermon, so she replied rather curtly, "I'm sure God, if there is a God, isn't interested in me. I haven't seen much evidence of His interest so far. And what makes you so sure that He has time to bother with my little problems, even if He does care for me?"

The older woman eagerly pursued the subject. "My dear girl, He not only cares for you, but He provided for your every need, even before you were born. He created you, just as He created Jesus, who lived among men and women, eating and sleeping as other men with one great difference. Jesus knew the source of His power and His supply, and He was amply cared for in every need." By this time, Jane was in place at the check-out counter and the cashier totaled her purchases and took her money. She forgot about the kindly woman behind her until she got to the door of the market; then she turned and smiled, remembering the comforting friendliness of the woman. On her short walk home, the woman's words began to sink in, and she found herself musing, "How would I feel if I really knew that God is with me, helping me, caring for me, bringing about better conditions in my life?" She found that she really wasn't as tired as she had been before her conversation with her helpful fellow shopper; as she went about her evening chores she began to imagine that God was with her, helping her with the work, giving her strength. She was more patient with the children and as she tucked them in for the night, she found a feeling of gratitude welling up within her. Silently she gave thanks for their health and her own, for the food they had enjoyed, for her good job. As she went down to join her husband she actually felt light-hearted. The very next day things began to change. The children actually offered to help with the evening chores, and they worked happily together. A few days later her husband came home with the exciting news that he had had a small promotion. Within just a few short weeks, Jane's life and the lives of her family were transformed . . . all through her new belief in God's love and provision, and her acceptance, in consciousness, of supply.

No person, place, thing or condition can keep your good from you. You may think that some person or some condition stands between you and your heart's desire; as long as you believe that to be true, it is. Nothing outside yourself denies you your good. Your own negative belief is the culprit. Deny that belief and replace it with a deep conviction in your good already manifested, and you will see that good flowing to you.

When you want water in your home, you do not stand in front of the faucet and command the water from the reservoir to come to you. No, you just turn the faucet and hold your cup under the flow of water. The water is already in the pipes, awaiting your action. So it is with supply. Your wealth is already in existence on the invisible side of life. As you accept it in consciousness, as you know it to be, you are turning the faucet and there is no further delay.

Are you thinking, "But I'm not a particularly religious person . . . will these ideas work for me?" Religion is not confined to a church, nor dependent upon one's following a particular creed. True religion is a deep belief in the goodness of God . . . faith in a power greater than one's human self . . . a feeling of oneness with the source of all good. Such a religion is the most practical idea in the world, and it produces practical results.

Your next remark might be, "But I know people who are not in any way religious, yet they prosper." Of course, we all know such people, but remember that true prosperity is not just money. It includes peace of mind, happiness, good relationships. What about your prosperous friends in those departments of life? True religion brings fantastic benefits to all facets of your life, not just in the form of money.

Prosperity doesn't depend entirely on the ability to get money. Some people believe that they can prosper only by taking from someone else. Some witty fellow once said:

There are two kinds of people—the takers and the givers. The takers eat well, but the givers sleep well.

Jesus' advice is still the best. "Seek ye first the kingdom of heaven [the feeling of inner harmony and peace] and all these things [food, clothing, houses, pleasure] shall be added unto you."

Prosperity is not a matter of thrift. Many penurious people are poor. Free spenders often get rich. Prosperity is often a matter of doing something which others fail to do, and doing it better.

Why do good, hardworking people often live such impoverished lives? Where is the justice? The answer is that we are working with the law of mind and expectancy. No matter how good a person may be, how seemingly deserving of life's blessings, it is DONE UNTO HIM AS HE BELIEVES: if he has a concept of "not enough to go around," he is actually scaring money away.

Now I want to ask you a question or two. How do you feel about yourself at this moment? Do you feel like a failure or a success? How do you feel about the world? Do you see life as something to endure and get through somehow, or do you see life as a wonderful, precious gift? How do you feel about the success of other people? When someone in your office or business is promoted, do you feel envy, or a genuine feeling of rejoicing with that person?

Why do you want to be prosperous?

Are you willing to make the necessary effort to think and act in a way that will result in prosperous living? Are you willing to give up some familiar, negative concepts and habits?

These questions may seem rather irrelevant in themselves, but the answers are very important. In fact, they can spell the difference between your being poor or prosperous. True prosperity is directly connected to your concepts of yourself and your world. Developing a healthy prosperity consciousness will not only bring more money into your life and experience, but it will change all other aspects of your beingness. Your health will improve, your relationships will be more harmonious, your work will be more satisfying, and life will take on a new glow. That's a promise!

Now can you accept the idea that God wants you to prosper? Can you really believe that you were created to succeed and to enjoy all the good things in life? Your very first step in realizing true prosperity in your life is to . . .

ESTABLISH IN YOUR MIND
YOUR RIGHT TO PROSPERITY.

Understand that money is a spiritual idea . . . a medium of exchange . . . a form of energy, and that back of all form there is a principle. The truth is that we live in a universe of abundance: there is no lack. This world did not produce itself. It didn't just happen and it did not produce the things that live upon it. The world and everything in it are expressions of the same system that produced it in the first place. There is a basic unity in all creation, and when you can grasp this important fact, you have taken the first real step toward true and lasting prosperity.

Prosperity is necessary for your spiritual growth and your well-being. Adequate financial supply gives you more time to pursue the finer things of life . . . hobbies, philanthropic endeavors, travel, further education.

A teacher who improved her life immeasurably through the practice of prosperity ideas said this: "I am a far better teacher since I discovered these laws. Prosperity has freed me to study and to travel, which in turn has increased my income even more and given me the greatest satisfaction I have ever known."

NOW TO THE PROCESS

1

Forgive and Release (the perfect cleanser)

Two things cannot occupy the same space at the same time; if your mind is cluttered with grudges, resentments, memories of past hurts and injustices, it cannot welcome new, fresh, prosperous ideas. Forgiveness is an absolute essential in the demonstration of prosperity.

A woman was fired from a very good job. Her first inclination was to write a nasty letter to her former employer, but she knew the law . . . that bitter, vindictive attitudes would only hurt her, not her boss. She knew that such ugly thoughts were a magnet for ugly conditions, so she wrote him a letter thanking him for his many kindnesses to her through the years. He was so touched by her thoughtfulness and understanding that he immediately called a competitor, highly recommending the woman for a similar position with another firm. The result was that within 24 hours the woman had a new job, at a higher salary and with greater benefits. Her forgiveness and understanding paid off in dollars and a more rewarding job.

Another woman was devastated when her husband of 25 years left her for another woman. She became a regular shrew when her husband came to visit the children.

She cried and pled with him to return. One day a friend told her about the power of forgiveness and release, and she began to work on herself and her attitudes. She found that her love for her husband was a very selfish and possessive one, and she began to realize why he had left. Each day she spent time releasing him mentally. She used this affirmation:

I NOW RELEASE YOU AND LET YOU GO TO YOUR HIGHEST GOOD. DIVINE LOVE IN ME IS THE MAGNET WHICH DRAWS ALL GOOD INTO MY LIFE NOW.

Of course she hoped that her husband was to be part of that good, but she truly released it all to God to work out in the best possible way. Her husband's visits became very pleasant for the whole family. She met him with a smile and kept the conversation light and cheerful; when he left, she sent him on his way with a smile. Gradually his visits grew in length. One day he took her into his arms, confessed that he had made a mistake in leaving, and asked for her forgiveness that he might come home to stay. Her possessiveness and her tears had only moved him to more resistance, but her gentle release had won him back.

Now begin to think of the things in your life that clutter it up . . . the used articles of clothing or household items that you no longer use. Don't wait for spring cleaning. Start now to clear out all items that you haven't worn or used in the last six months. I do this regularly and it is such fun! I can hardly wait to see what is coming to replace the things I give away. Load up your car and head for the nearest thrift shop. Your cast-off things can be just what someone else is looking for. This practice always brings good results because it is involved with the principle of circulation.

STEPS IN THE CLEANSING PROCESS:

- Spend a few minutes at night and in the morning breathing deeply, breathing out fear, worry, and tension . . . breathing in freedom, ease, joy and love, feeling your oneness with God and with all life.

- Begin to eliminate from your life what you do not want or need, beginning with the forgiveness of the following people who have irritated you the most:

  _____

  _____

  _____

- Affirm several times a day, *naming* the individuals in this statement, speaking with feeling and sincerity:

  I FORGIVE YOU FULLY AND COMPLETELY. ALL IS WELL BETWEEN US FROM THIS MOMENT ON.

- Next, think of the things you are willing to release from your life and write them here:

  _____

  _____

  _____

- Affirm with feeling:

  I RELEASE YOU TO YOUR NEW OWNER WITH JOY. THERE IS NOW ROOM FOR NEWER, FINER ITEMS WHICH I AM READY TO RECEIVE WITH APPRECIATION.

- Finally, list the conditions or attitudes you no longer want in your life, such as jealousy, anger, inharmony, frustration:

_____

_____

_____

Follow this release with these words:

MY WORLD AND EVERYTHING AND EVERY-ONE IN IT IS NOW IN DIVINE ORDER. THANK YOU.

2

Watch Your Words, Actions and Reactions

What is your position when the office staff gathers for lunch or just conversation and the subject turns to the affairs of the world—inflation, crime, pollution or any of the other cheery topics of conversation which seem to dominate our attention these days? Do you chime right in with the prophets of doom, adding your energy and attention to the problem? Or do you contribute some positive comment, not meant to antagonize, but to lift the level of the conversation?

Later, at your desk do you find yourself going over the negative remarks you have heard or read, feeling a sense

of futility about doing anything really significant concerning the conditions? Did you ever get a bill in the mail and immediately begin to worry over it? Perhaps you talked over your worry with your mate or your friend, all the time working up more feeling about the lack of money to meet the bill. This is the gestation period. The child or result (the offspring of your worried thought and feeling) will be more worry and even an inability to demonstrate money for other, simpler wants. Illness often results from this kind of prolonged anxiety.

You have the power to choose what shall find a welcome home in your mind. You do not always have the ability to choose what your ears hear, but you can decide what you will let into your consciousness, what you will feel deeply. We are all so vulnerable to the news media. We are all susceptible to the insidious influences all around us, and we all carry on silent dialogues with ourselves most of the time. What do you say to yourself when you are alone? Do you find yourself asking, "How will I make ends meet with prices going up so alarmingly?" or "What security is there in such a world?" If you have had such questions, whether they are verbally expressed or not, your responsibility is to begin to BE AWARE of your thoughts, your actions and your reactions to outside stimuli. Instead of saying, "I can't afford that," substitute this thought: "I choose not to buy this today." Instantly, you will lose the feeling of deprivation. You have made a choice. Remember, there is only one Source—God. People, jobs, investments, are simply channels for the delivery of God's good into your life. God is totally unaffected by changing conditions and fluctuating economies. When you find yourself giving way to fear and negative thinking and feeling, immediately replace that thought with a statement such as this:

GOD IS THE ONLY PRESENCE AND THE ONLY POWER IN MY LIFE. ALL IS WELL!

Mike Todd said: "Being broke is a temporary condition. Being poor is a mental condition. I've been broke lots of times, but I've never been poor."

If you are working in a business or organization and are privately feeling that you are unappreciated and underpaid, you are subconsciously severing your ties with that organization. You have set a law into motion. When the manager says, "We'll have to let you go," he is simply the instrument through which your own negative mental state is being confirmed.

During World War II, a self-righteous, proud, churchgoing woman feared that through rationing she would not get her share of coffee, so she bought up all she could and hid it away in her basement. One Sunday when she returned from church she found that burglars had broken into her house and taken all her jewelry, silver . . . and coffee. She wailed, "Why did this happen to me when I was at church? I'm a good woman and I never stole from anyone." Was she not in the consciousness of fear and lack when she began to hoard? She had set into motion a law. Through the quality of her thinking she attracted the outer action which conformed to her inner thinking and feeling.

A housewife was terribly crippled with arthritis and her condition failed to respond to any medical attention. In a conversation with her minister, she admitted that she had hated her dead husband for more than 30 years. Her anger and hostility couldn't affect him at all, of course, but her attitudes were slowly killing her.

Phineas Quimby said this: "The suggestion you give another, you are giving yourself. This is the reason that the Golden Rule is a Cosmic Divine Law." Quimby knew that when one entertains negative thoughts of envy, greed or vindictiveness, he is hurting himself because he is the one thinking and feeling such destructive thoughts.

3

Condition Your Mind to Get Ready
for New Waves of Abundance

I suggest that you begin this very pleasant discipline by purchasing an inexpensive concordance. Then, with your concordance and Bible in hand, begin to look up all the words concerned with supply, money, abundance, wealth. You want to develop a new vocabulary filled with words which bring to mind (and experience) the richness you want in your life.

Years ago in a class on prosperity, students were asked to do this and I won the prize! I had 73 words, some of which I made up out of other words, but they were accepted by the instructor, and it was such a "fun" exercise.

The word "abundance" means "to rise up in waves" and this is exactly what will happen as you start to work with these new words. You will find your conversation sparked with words which will interest others. You will be sought out by others who don't know exactly why they always feel good when you are around (but you'll know, and your magnetism and charm will increase daily as your prosperity is also increasing!).

Spend time looking at expensive things . . . fine cars, lovely clothing, beautiful homes. You do not look at them longingly, but gratefully, rejoicing in the joy and happiness they bring their owners, knowing that you can demonstrate your own fine things.

For several years, every time my husband and I were on our way home from a concert or meeting or family gathering, we would drive past the showroom which displayed expensive cars . . . Jaguars, Rolls Royces and Bentleys. My husband chose one Jaguar and found a brochure describing its many fine features. Every time we visited that showroom he found something else desirable on the model car; in between times he saturated his mind with the now-familiar fine qualities of the car. Of course in a very short time we had that exact model . . . not from the showroom floor with the high price tag, but one which came to us in a most remarkable way . . . literally from the proverbial "little old lady in Pasadena." My husband had conditioned his mind to accept that particular car; later, he acquired several airplanes in just the same way.

The power of the spoken word cannot be emphasized too strongly. *By thy words shalt thou be justified, and by thy words thou shalt be condemned. Matthew 12:37*

One way to prepare your mind is through the use of AFFIRMATIONS. An affirmation is simply a statement of Truth, repeated over and over until it becomes a part of one's total feeling and thinking. The word literally "becomes flesh." How often have you said over and over, "I am sick . . . there isn't enough money to meet the bills this month . . . why are things so tight for us?" Do you realize that in those statements you are using the power of affirmation? You are affirming (making firm in your experience) something which you surely do not want. You are giving power, unconsciously, but surely, to adverse conditions; the more you indulge in these negative thoughts, the worse you feel. For just a few moments, think about these statements:

THE LORD IS MY SHEPHERD. I WANT FOR NOTH-ING. GOD IS THE ONLY POWER IN MY LIFE, AND HE IS BRINGING INTO MY EXPERIENCE RIGHT NOW EVERYTHING WHICH IS FOR MY HIGHEST GOOD.

Say these words over to yourself for a few minutes . . . feel them . . . say them with emotion and with your total attention. Now, how do you feel? Lighter, more like smiling? Through these words you are connected with the One source . . . you are part of the flow of universal good . . . you are in touch with the real self of you, that part of you made in the image and likeness of God.

One very simple, powerful affirmation consists of just three words:

I AM PROSPERITY.

In a recent class on the subject of successful living, the instructor asked the students to repeat these words 50 times each day; the results were startling. One man reported: "It's absolutely uncanny the way things began to change. When I started to worry over bills, when my sinus condition began to act up, when my mother-in-law came to stay for 3 months in our six-room house, I just said to myself,

I AM PROSPERITY. THIS IS THE NEW THOUGHT HABIT OF MY LIFE. I WILL THINK ONLY HEALTH, HAPPINESS AND PROSPERITY.

This man went on to say that after he began his practice of saying this affirmation over 50 times each day, he discovered, on the second day, that one simple food eliminated from his diet would also eliminate his sinus trouble; his income tax refund was several hundred dollars more than he had expected; his mother-in-law got so interested in his new attitude that she began to attend classes with him, and a new very pleasant relationship was established between them.

What new good do you want to bring into your life? Why not try this method? As you say the words I AM PROSPERITY, think about what you are saying. Feel the words deeply. Thrill to them. Thank God for them. Begin to tie them in to several commonplace, everyday actions. Speak the words when you get into your car . . . when you unlock your door . . . when you open your mail . . . when you dress for the day . . . while you are waiting for the traffic signal to turn green.

If you will follow these simple instructions intelligently and faithfully for seven days, you, too, will be amazed at the beneficial changes that will take place in your life.

Another way to prepare your mind is through the POWER OF BLESSING.

We usually think of the act of blessing particularly at Thanksgiving time, but the practice of bestowing blessings on people, conditions and things should be a way of life. As presented in the book of Genesis, the act of blessing was the favorite form of prayer among the Hebrew people, who considered a blessing to be a priceless gift. The Lord pointed out the power of blessing to Abraham when He said, "I will bless thee and make thy name great, and thou shalt be a blessing." Jacob considered a blessing such a desirable thing that he stole the blessing which his father had intended to grant to his brother Esau.

To bless means to make holy or whole by spoken words. It means to ask divine favor for some situation or condition. To bless is to wish a person or a situation well, to gladden, to glorify, to praise. To bless means to behold the good, and, in this recognition, to bring forth the quality of goodness in a person or condition. How often we have condemned, criticized, or cursed a situation, bringing forth more problems, when we could have dared to take the opposite view, blessing the situation, thereby

31

activating the omnipresent good within it, resulting in a happy solution.

Blessing is a most important part of your prosperity program, so begin right now to bless everything that comes into your life. Use these words of blessing (particularly helpful for bringing harmony into discordant conditions):

I BLESS YOU AND PRAISE YOU FOR THE GOOD- NESS OF GOD THAT IS WITHIN YOU!

You will find that merchandise which has not moved from the shelves will be sold easily, as many successful merchants have demonstrated, through the use of this affirmation:

I BLESS YOU RIGHT NOW WITH IMMEDIATE SELLING POWER.

If you are a business person, begin to bless your employees, as well as your service or product. One merchant found this practice of blessing so powerful that he reported a tripling of his sales in less than two months.

Use the word of blessing in collecting money that is due you. One man to whom a large sum of money had been owed for several years, heard about this method of bringing about right and just action, and he used this affirmation every night before going to sleep:

I BLESS YOU AND PRAISE YOU FOR THE GOOD- NESS OF GOD, WORKING IN AND THROUGH YOU RIGHT NOW.

After just three nights of this kind of mental and

spiritual release, the man owing him called to say that he was mailing a check for the entire amount. After months of demanding letters, worrisome, resentful thoughts, the perfect result finally came as the simple practice of blessing and praising was employed.

Emmet Fox, that great Truth teacher, said this about blessing: *Bless a thing and it will bless you. Curse it and it will curse you. If you put your condemnation on anything in life, it will hit back at you and hurt you. If you bless a situation, it has no power to hurt you, and even if it is troublesome for a time, it will gradually fade out if you sincerely bless it.*

Of course, blessing the body has often been proved to be the most effective way of handling physical challenges. Use this powerful statement many times a day:

I AM GRATEFUL THAT MY BODY IS THE TEMPLE OF THE LIVING GOD. I BLESS, PRAISE, AND GIVE THANKS FOR DIVINE HEALTH IN AND THROUGH MY BODY AND ALL OF ITS FUNCTIONS.

Bless the traffic as you drive the crowded highways and watch the way made clear for you. Bless your money, your debts, your problems, your food, your body, your family, your business, your friends. You can improve every condition in your life by blessing it. Could anything be simpler? Try it!

Relax and say to yourself several times a day:

MONEY IS CONSTANTLY CIRCULATING IN MY LIFE. I AM BLESSED AND PROSPERED IN ALL THINGS.

As you do this regularly and systematically, the idea of wealth will be conveyed to your deeper mind and you will begin to develop a "wealth" consciousness. You must *feel* the truth of what you affirm. Remember that thought and feeling must be wed to each other. No "child" (result) can come forth without this union.

At first your conscious mind may entirely reject the statement, I AM WEALTHY NOW. Your conscious mind argues back, "You are not and you know it." If you find this conflict going on between what you want and what you have previously conditioned yourself to expect, say something like this:

EVERY DAY MY WEALTH IS INCREASING . . .or
. . . EVERY DAY MY SALES ARE INCREASING IN MARVELOUS WAYS.

This idea your mind can totally accept, and later you can go on to the absolute and authoritative statement, I AM WEALTHY NOW. (This idea is psychologically convincing and acceptable to your conscious mind. Such statements are identifying with truth that is eternal, changeless, and timeless.)

A businessman, puzzled because he had been out of work so long, went to his minister for help. He said, "I have been a faithful member of this church for years. I have read all the books on positive thinking . . . where have I gone wrong? What can I do, or not do, to bring prosperity into my life?" His minister asked, "What kind of silent conversations have you been carrying on with yourself?" The man admitted that he had been rehashing all the negatives in his life . . . can't find a job . . . no money . . . hopeless future . . . a failure. You might say that he was filled with negative positives, convinced as he was of his failure. The minister then advised the man to begin to repeat some prosperity affirmations, to which the man replied, "I can't be bothered with the silly repetition of a few words. That's kid stuff." But the minister insisted. Within two weeks the man had been offered the best position of his career. In a letter to his minister he said this: "I will never again doubt the power of the spoken word. Now I know that it just isn't enough to attend church and read all the helpful books. The vocal expressions of positive thoughts, charged with sincere feeling turned the tide for me. There is tremendous power in the spoken word!"

Each one of us can be a positive influence for good in our homes, our businesses, our schools, throughout the community and the world by realizing that depressions and recessions and troubled times are man's creation. The eternal is still eternal. God is still God and in complete control of His world, no matter what the appearances. Jesus said, "Be in the world, but not of it." The truth is that we are spiritual beings living on this planet earth for a few short years, but we are eternal beings right now. Conditions can be good or bad, but God *is*. I believe with all my heart that God is still trying to express His power and His good through people, and that even God can't open new channels of blessing and supply when the mind and feelings are clogged with fear and distrust and a sense of futility.

Spend time each day with the Bible and its promises, at the same time that you are living in a world of appearances and constant change. "The Lord is my shepherd, I shall not want," wrote the shepherd-king, David. The word "Lord" also means "Law" and the law is that whatever you believe shall be done unto you. The Lord (law) is that upon which you can depend, no matter what the conditions. If you know the law, you can live at peace with yourself and your fellow man, living with the restrictions of a tight economy, but more aware of your source than you are of the changing conditions around you. This is true freedom, and it comes from looking only to God for everything in your life.

STEPS TO MORE PROSPEROUS THINKING:

- Make a list of "prosperous" words. Add at least two new prospering words to your vocabulary each day. Use them at least five times each day, even if you have to talk to yourself. You are the one you are most interested in prospering, so don't be apologetic or shy about using these powerful words in your silent conversations in your own mind!

- Repeat the phrase "I AM PROSPERITY" 50 times a day.

4

Be Flexible, Open and Receptive

When you begin to be exposed to new ideas about prosperity, many of your old concepts will be challenged. It isn't easy to give up notions and opinions and attitudes which have been years in the building, but remember that those old ideas are responsible for your sense of lack and limitation, so they must go!

As you begin to work with these new, prosperous ideas, keep your mind open to newness. You are embarking on an exciting adventure, one which will increase in benefits and blessings for as long as you live, so enter into this new experience with eagerness and anticipation.

Jesus talked about the futility of pouring new wine into old bottles. He was talking about trying to put new ideas into old forms which had long outgrown their usefulness. As long as you remain static and fixed in your ideas, even God cannot bring into your life the blessings you want. So be like a little child—wide-eyed and interested in the world around you. God is full of wonderful surprises and you will be blind to them if you are not alert and expectant.

In the first Beatitude Jesus says, "Blessed are the poor in spirit, for theirs is the kingdom of God!" The word "poor" has not been rightly understood. It does not mean that one is to be impoverished and needy, but rather that one is to be open, teachable, flexible. Remember that prosperity is not just money. It is happiness, health, well-being, and it is also ideas. There is no shortage of money in this universe, just a shortage of people who are open to the fantastic new ideas literally floating in the ethers waiting to be picked up by some alert, inquisitive mind.

A church was having financial problems and the board called in a financial expert who shocked its members by saying, "You do not have a financial problem, but you do have an idea problem. You haven't done anything new and innovative around here in 20 years. One good idea could generate enough income to clear away all your seeming financial problems." After the expert's visit, the board members had a brain-storming session; one man admitted that many good ideas had come before them and all had been promptly shelved as being "risky" or "too different" or "too much of a departure from the way we've always done it." The members decided that they were going to be open and receptive to newness, so they adopted two new ideas for expansion; within just three months not only were their financial troubles over, but new people were flocking to services and to the new activities.

In the book of Isaiah we read these words, "Behold I will do a new thing; now it shall spring forth and you shall know it. I will even make a way in the wilderness and rivers in the desert." This is God's way of saying that even in the dry, parched areas of our lives, He can bring forth lush abundance; but it will be a new thing, not built on the old concepts and ideas.

Is it difficult for you to accept newness? Begin today to practice doing things a different way. If you always get out of bed on the left side, tomorrow morning, get out on the other side. If you always read the financial page of the paper first, read the weather, the news, or the back pages where all the encouraging human-interest stories are hidden. When you find yourself getting tense over your son's long hair, stop and ask yourself whether this situation is worth your anger and frustration. When the church bulletin announces a new order of service with some new songs you have never heard, rejoice in this opportunity to learn something new, to flow with the changes, which must be right for someone or they would not have been made. Actually this exercise in flexibility and openness can be fun. It's amazing what creatures of habit we are! You have heard the description of a rut, I am sure. It is a grave with both ends knocked out!

Wake up to newness. Learn to savor the moment with all of its infinite possibilities which you will miss entirely if you are not open, receptive and flexible.

LEARN TO USE YOUR IMAGINATION CONSTRUCTIVELY

If you have ever said to yourself, "I have no imagination," think again. What were your thoughts the night your daughter was late getting home? Didn't you imagine all sorts of things that might be happening? Or where was your mental attention when you found that your job might be terminated? Wasn't your mind filled with dreadful possibilities? You were using your imagination, but in a destructive, negative way. Now I am suggesting that you begin to use your imagination for what you want, not for what you don't want.

Think of one of your goals or one of your objectives. How would you feel if it were already a reality? How would you feel if you were on the plane, on your way to that fabulous vacation spot? Wouldn't you be bubbling with joy and anticipation? I have discovered that one of the secrets of accomplishing my goals is to "act as if." I spend time getting into the feeling of the thing already visible or manifest. For example, if a trip is my objective, I spend time picturing my arrival at my destination. I "see" my friends or relatives greeting me . . . I hear the laughter, the chatter, and "feel" the joy of being with people I love. If the objective is the acquisition of something new, I picture myself enjoying it . . . the pleasure of driving down the street in my new car, or the satisfaction of wearing some new article of clothing, or the joy and fulfillment of seeing a new program prosper and succeed. The secret is to "feel" the thing already accomplished. Remember that thought alone is not enough. Thought must be combined with deep, sincere feeling and emotion.

STEPS TO GET YOU OUT OF THE RUT:

- Each day do at least three things in a totally different way.

- Read Emerson's essay "CIRCLES"! You will come to realize that you can never reach the limit of your own potential. Your good is inexhaustible. This belief should be part of your very being.

I AM OPEN AND RECEPTIVE TO ALL THE GOOD GOD HAS IN STORE FOR ME.

5

Begin to Absorb from the Universe

When a seed is planted in the ground it begins to absorb from the soil all that it needs to nurture it. It receives moisture and nutriments from the soil; then it absorbs the rays of the sun, the air. It is the nature of the plant to operate in this way, and it has no volition of its own. Man, on the other hand, has the power of choice. You live in a universe of abundance, but unless you know it, and choose to cooperate with it, it is useless to you. You are part of the universe. Every phase of nature's laws applies to you in some way, including the law of absorption; so begin today to absorb some of the beauty around you. Take time to listen to good music . . . read an uplifting book . . . smell the flowers . . . appreciate a friend . . . spend time with these ideas which will nurture your spiritual nature.

A sponge immersed in water becomes completely saturated with the water . . . it returns to the state of complete oneness with the environment in which it grew. So man, in returning to his Source, abiding in it, reaches the point of complete saturation where he sees himself as one with it in all things.

Years ago in the early days of our marriage, we lived in a small southern army town, and money was scarce. I planned our simple meals around what money we could save out of our tiny allowance. Thursdays were shopping days, and on his way home from the airfield my husband would stop at the PX for our week's supply of groceries. We had eaten split pea soup for days, and my mouth was watering for some delicacy that hot Thursday night as I waited for him to come home. He came in the back door of our little rented house, put down a small bag of groceries, then handed me a bunch of rather wilted violets which he had bought with some of the precious grocery money. I was furious! "But what about some good food for a change," I blurted out. He quietly replied, "There are times when violets are more important." Later as we ate our simple supper, the revived violets and a couple of candles in wedding-gift crystal holders added a lovely touch of grace and beauty to our table. He was right. Sometimes violets are more important than food. That night our souls were fed as well as our bodies.

As you begin to be aware of that part of your God-given supply which is free for the taking and enjoying, you will find much of your hunger for the finer things being filled. So many beautiful things in life are free . . . gorgeous sunsets . . . breath-takingly spectacular sunrises . . . trees . . . flowers . . . a child's smile . . . a garden path after a spring rain . . . a good book . . . music . . . art . . . the list goes on and on.

One of the early metaphysical writers said that desire is God saying to you, "Here is the good you desire. It is only an idea now, but through your acceptance of it (absorption) as an idea, it becomes reality. Dare to accept it now." Remember that you are not trying to get something that belongs to someone else. You are a child of God, and therefore you inherit all that He has prepared for you before you were even born.

For me, the music of Bach, Mozart and Schubert have always epitomized order and an inner harmony. Whenever I need a sense of order, a kind of inner nourishment, I play recordings of the works of those composers, and soon my mind is again functioning in an orderly, efficient manner. I also find that whenever I am in Hawaii, with all its incomparable charms, there is this same sense of inner nourishment.

STEPS TO OPEN YOUR LIFE TO BEAUTY

- Open yourself to at least three lovely, harmonious experiences each day . . . listen to some beautiful music, read some poetry or prose that uplifts and inspires you . . . look for and enjoy a picture of something beautiful—a glorious sunrise or sunset, a child's open, upturned face. Take time to enjoy, to experience the beauty deep within you.

6

Develop Your Love-Ability

Fifty years ago people lived in tight-knit communities. There were always grandparents, aunts, uncles and cousins nearby to give support and love. Today in our mobile society, loneliness and a sense of isolation is very real to many people; there is a desperate need for love, expressed and demonstrated.

Just as is the case with enthusiasm, so it is true that nothing really worthwhile is ever achieved without love. Learning to love and express that love is an absolute essential in demonstrating prosperity. Love softens and melts the hard places in our hearts. It makes us more aware of the needs of others. Love opens us to more opportunities and possibilities than does any other emotion.

Jesus said, "By this shall all men know that you are my disciples, if you have love one to another." He didn't say that disciples would be recognized because of what they had accomplished or accumulated, but by the degree of love they expressed to the world.

The great Mahatma Gandhi once said, "A single person who has achieved supreme love is sufficient to nullify the hatred of millions."

Love is an energy. Scientists today are discovering that to live as if life and love were one is an indispensible condition because this is the way of life which the real nature of man demands. The idea is not new. What is new is that we should be discovering, by scientific means, the ancient truths of the Sermon on the Mount.

In the book of Matthew, where we are given a description of judgment day, the test of man is not, "How have you believed?" but rather "How have you loved?"

Who seeks for heaven alone to save his soul
May keep the path, but not reach the goal.
While he who walks in love may wander far
Yet God will bring him where the blessed are.

STEPS TO BRING LOVE INTO YOUR LIFE:

- Read the 13th chapter of 1st Corinthians twice each day for one month, morning and night. You will find that each time you read it, there will be new meaning and new understanding of the words and how they are becoming part of your new prosperous consciousness.

7

Love Your Work

The way you feel about your work is a major key in your ability to feel and experience prosperity. It is true that your income may come through channels other than your work; by work we mean whatever occupies your time and energy, whether that includes a salary or not. You are here to express God through your particular talents and abilities.

There is a story about a man who died and found himself in a beautiful place, surrounded by every conceivable comfort. A white-jacketed man came to him and said, "You may have anything you choose . . . any food . . . any pleasure . . . any kind of entertainment." The man was delighted, and for days he sampled all the delicacies and experiences of which he had dreamed while on earth. But one day he grew bored with all of it and, calling the attendant to him, he said, "I'm tired of all this. I need something to do. What kind of work can you give me to do?" The attendant sadly shook his head and replied, "I'm sorry, sir. That's the one thing we can't do for you. There is no work here for you." The man answered, "That's a fine thing. I might as well be in hell!" The attendant said softly, "Where do you think you are?"

Do you ever think how fortunate you are if you have work that you enjoy and that gives you a sense of well-being and purpose? If your work doesn't evoke that kind of response in you, one of two things should be considered. Either you can look for another job, or you can set to work finding ways to make your present job more rewarding and interesting. But do *something!*

Emerson knew the key when he said, "Whatever you do, let your work be organic." Emerson knew the importance of putting one's whole self into any project or undertaking.

It may not be your job that is the problem, but your attitude toward that job. What can you do to make it the kind of satisfying work everyone seeks? You can put more energy and time and interest in it. You can find a need and fill it. You can learn to love what you are doing when you come to understand that all work is noble and enriching when it is performed in a spirit of love and good will and with a desire to serve.

"He profits most who serves best." This is a living truth. Follow it and you will find a mysterious change taking place in you. At first you may have been trying to get something. Now the very thing you are seeking is also seeking you. It is the other side of the coin. There comes a feeling that you are not only making progress, but you are also in harmony with the universe.

As you come to the realization that work is for the purpose of developing and expressing skill and ability, there will be no more drudgery in your labors. Your attitude toward your work is all-important. Give grudgingly and you'll receive grudgingly.

You know the story of the three brick masons. When the first man was asked what he was building, he answered gruffly, without even raising his eyes from his work, "I'm laying bricks." The second man replied, "I'm building a wall." But the third man said enthusiastically and with obvious pride, "I'm building a cathedral."

What are you building? A day-to-day existence or a happy, successful, prosperous life? There is a difference.

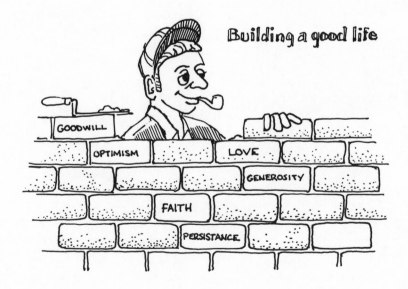

Building a good life

STEPS TO FINDING JOY IN YOUR JOB

- Find at least one thing each day that you can do to improve your work.

- Look for ways of perfecting some task, and for opportunities to be of more service to those with whom you work.

8

Plan Your Work, Then Work Your Plan

This phase of your prosperity program is lots of fun! It is involved with goal setting and reaching those goals in interesting and varied ways. If you are content to drift from day to day, without any definite goals or plans for advancement, you will become the victim of circumstances. You will be pushed this way and that by the events over which you seem to have no control. You will always be subject to the opinions and actions of others. Remember that you always have the power of choice. As someone has said, "If you can't decide, you have decided." You have decided to be indecisive.

Begin to set several different kinds of goals . . . some small, relatively easy and comfortable goals for the next day, and some more extensive and long-range ones. I set goals for the day, the week, the month and the year. Lists are a way of life for me and I heartily recommend the practice of list-making. Such a practice frees your mind to handle the really important issues.

Many years ago the famous steel magnate Charles Schwab reputedly paid a friend $25,000 for a simple idea which worked so well that it was worth that much to Mr. Schwab and his associates and employees. The idea was just this: Make a list of the six most important things to do each day, and cross them off as they are accomplished.

Do not overlook the value of writing. It impresses the subconscious mind at another level.

GOALS

In setting your goals, be sure to exercise good judgment and common sense. If you can't possibly conceive of yourself having a million dollars, you would be foolish to list it as one of your monthly goals. Choose an amount which you can accept in consciousness. Ask yourself these questions, using them as guidelines for all of your goals:

- Does this thing or condition exist?
- Can I believe in its existing for me?
- Is it right for me and for everyone concerned?
- Can it be accomplished well, in new and innovative ways?
- Is it for the glory of God and the good of all people?

For example, you know that a million dollars exists, but can you see yourself having that amount . . . can you visualize how you would handle it, what complications it might bring? Will your desire not bring harm or loss to anyone? Remember that any gain at another's expense is not in accordance with God's laws. There is enough and to spare in God's opulent universe.

One little tip in your goal-setting. Always leave room for God's idea of your good. You may be limiting yourself without realizing it.

Years ago I wanted one hundred dollars for a particular item for our home. I prayed and treated for that amount every day for weeks and one day my mother said to me, "Honey, I have been thinking about giving you a gift for you to use any way you choose, so here is $100.00." I was ecstatic. "It works! It works!" I was shouting inwardly. Then came the shocker, and a lesson I have never forgotten. My mother went on, "It's strange; I had intended to make this check for $500, but something kept telling me $100 . . . $100." You can believe that from that day to this, I have said, "This is what I desire, Father, but you know best—so this or something better."

God's idea of good

My idea of good

57

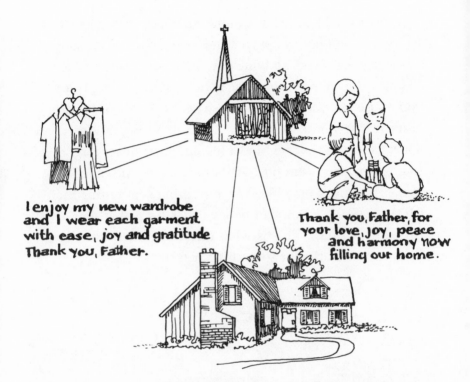

I enjoy my new wardrobe
and I wear each garment
with ease, joy and gratitude
Thank you, Father.

Thank you, Father, for
your love, joy, peace
and harmony now
filling our home.

I thank God for our lovely home, just
right in every detail, and for ample supply
to maintain it in order and beauty.

Prosperity Blueprint

9

Prosperity Blueprint

When you want to build a new home or a patio or even a new flower garden, you have a plan. If it is a house you are building, you need a very detailed blueprint, giving every minute detail, with all specifications precise and accurate. In just the same way, a new life is first set forth in visible form on paper. This is sometimes called treasure mapping . . . I like the term Prosperity Blueprint. It could also be called "pictured prayer." It is a road map with guidelines for our thinking and feeling as we move toward the manifestation of the good we desire. A Prosperity Blueprint is a piece of paper on which we place pictures of what we want with statements of faith accompanying each picture.

Your prosperity blueprint may be a large wall map. It may be a small notebook or a leaf in a book. Whatever form you choose, it is a means of keeping your attention on what you want. It gives direction and definition to your desires.

Making a prosperity blueprint is in itself an act of faith, the first step in demonstration. It says, in effect: "Father, I know that you love me. As the giver of every good and perfect gift I know you have already provided all the good that is rightfully mine as your beloved child. Through this blueprint, I am declaring that I am now ready to receive my highest good, under grace, in perfect ways. I thank you.''

Some people believe that it is wrong to pray for things (and there is a higher way, which we will discuss later), but we must walk before we can run; making blueprints for prosperity is a step toward the time when we ask for nothing, but simply are open to receive all that the Father has for us. We believe that Jesus meant it when He said, ''I came that you might have life and have it more abundantly.'' We also believe that *abundantly* means just that—life filled with material good as well as spiritual riches. We are rich sons and daughters of God, and blueprinting for prosperity helps us to realize our rich heritage.

I could tell you countless stories of people who have used this exciting and effective way of bringing desired good into their lives. I have made several blueprints in the past, and without exception, they have been totally successful. My most thrilling adventure began many years ago when I wanted to move from our comfortable, large house, which was a joy in most ways, but which required a great deal of upkeep and plain hard work.

I saw a beautiful, Oriental-style home in the Sunday magazine section of the paper one day. It had a swimming pool, guest house, tea house, exquisitely manicured gardens, and it sounded as if it might be adequate for our needs. I cut the picture out of the magazine, put it on my first prosperity blueprint, tacked it on my closet door (inside) and thought no more about it until one hot Sunday a few weeks later. Driving home from a friend's house, I noticed a "For Sale" sign on the lawn of an ordinary-looking house, just a few blocks from our home. I had time, so I decided to have a look—just for fun. I had driven past half a dozen other houses with "For Sale" signs but something seemed to draw me to this one. The real estate agent met me at the front door, and as she led me toward the back of the house my heart nearly stopped. Through the sliding glass doors at the rear of the large living room I could see the garden beyond . . . and the tea house . . . and the pool . . . and the guest house. It couldn't be, and yet it was—the house on my blueprint!

It was just as the newspaper article had described it, but lovelier and more inviting. I called my husband, who came right up to see it; he, too, loved it on sight, but being the practical member of our team he said, "But honey, we *have* a home. Where are we going to get the $6,000 for the down payment? I'll admit this place has everything we need and want, but we have to look at facts." Of course, I knew that he was right, from his viewpoint, but there was my blueprint! This was our new home and I was absolutely sure of it. He finally gave in and said we'd make an offer and put our house on the market the very next day. That night I went to sleep in the old house, but in my imagination I was in the new one, looking from the bedroom out into the moonlit garden with the peaceful pool and huge deodar trees making strange shadows on the water.

The next day before the children were off to school, an old friend whom we hadn't heard from in months, called and said, "I am transferring some funds from one account to another, and I wondered if you would have any use for $6,000 for 60 days?" I could hardly speak. When my voice returned, I told her about the new house, and then arranged to meet her at her bank that afternoon. Before my husband came home that night, the six thousand dollars was in our bank account and we wrote out the check for the deposit on the new house. The financing went through without a problem, and we lived in that lovely home for six happy years . . . until we needed a home in a different location, nearer to our work. I believe in blueprinting for prosperity and success!

Not only can one make a blueprint for things, but for conditions, for increase in business, for harmonious relationships. Try it!

A man in an eastern city lost his job and, having heard about this way of visually accepting desired good, he made his blueprint. He knew exactly the kind of job he wanted and where he wanted it to be. He found a picture in a magazine of the kind of office where he wanted to work, and he set to work making his blueprint. Under the pictures he wrote these words:

I WORK FOR GOD. HE NEEDS ME IN THIS JOB OR A BETTER ONE. HE LOVES ME AND ALWAYS PRO-VIDES JUST WHAT I NEED WHEN I NEED IT.

His boldness startled him, but the very next day, looking at his blueprint, he suddenly decided to go back to a firm that had previously interviewed him. The personnel clerk asked him to fill in one blank he had left empty on his earlier visit. Quickly he wrote in the salary he expected. At the moment he would have settled for half the amount, but for some reason he wrote in the larger figure. That afternoon he had a call from the personnel manager asking him to come to work the next day. Later the manager said to him, "I liked the decisiveness with which you wrote in the amount of salary you wanted. That kind of authority and confidence and self-esteem is just what we need in this position."

A blueprint keeps all activity of your mind and emotions going forward without wasted time, motion, and emotion. It is another form of goal-setting, and one which seems to work quickly and successfully.

A few hints concerning your adventure with your blueprint: KEEP IT TO YOURSELF! Nothing can dissipate energy more quickly than some well-meaning friend's skeptical view of your exciting project. Of course, if husband and wife can agree completely on some objective, or if there is a team feeling and common interest in a group, it is helpful to have more than one person working on the goals at once; but make sure that those with whom you share your ideas are completely in harmony with those ideas. If in doubt, keep them to yourself.

And of course, a cardinal rule is that you never, never make goals or blueprints for someone else, except in generalities . . . for example, you would be perfectly safe in blueprinting an education for your child, but don't be so specific as to name the school or what your child will study. We have no right to interfere with another's free will, even that of our children or mates.

One woman blueprinted for a husband who unfortunately happened to be married to her best friend. She worked hard, and even had a snapshot of the man on her blueprint. She got him after a very painful and disastrous divorce, and then discovered that he was as unfaithful to her as he had been to his former wife. Never be specific in naming a particular person in your plan. Keep it general. You would be wise to include in your blueprint a picture of a happy couple, perhaps with these words under the picture:

I GIVE THANKS FOR MY PERFECT MATE, ONE WHO IS RIGHT FOR ME AS I AM RIGHT FOR HIM.

Another very important point concerning this "fun" way of bringing prosperity into your life: Let it be just that—fun! Don't be too intense. The light touch is always the sure touch. Artists have it, good cooks have it, and in praying, the light touch is also important. When we can pray lightly, we know that our prayers are effective. God responds to the lightest of thoughts, the softest of whispers, the gentlest of feelings. We cannot have the light touch until we are free from doubt. Praying, visualizing, planning with the light touch indicates that we are no longer trying to convince ourselves of God.

Most of us have the "hard work" consciousness. Haven't you ever said, "I've been praying hard about it"? Success is often equated with hard work. When Adam and Eve were driven out of the Garden of Eden, they were told by God, "All thy days shalt thou labor by the sweat of thy brow." They had fallen from belief in God as all supply and had accepted two powers. Man has been working hard ever since; while hard work often brings success, it also often brings ulcers, broken marriages and unhappiness in general. There is no true prosperity unless the bank account is accompanied by health and happiness. Prosperity must involve the whole person.

A woman and her family were forced to move when her husband was transferred to another community. She knew the law and didn't panic. Instead she went about her daily tasks with a light heart, affirming often:

OUR NEW HOME IS READY FOR US. WE FIND IT WITHOUT DELAY, AND IT IS PERFECT.

The light touch worked quickly. Within two days, she had indeed found the perfect home, and the person who had given her the lead about the house was the very woman who eventually bought hers!

Your blueprint should be simple, with clear, vivid pictures in color. Color helps to focus attention and we remember colors easily. I would use a pink background when blueprinting for health, a deeper pink or rose red if my need was for more love. Bright green or gold seem to be most in keeping when you are blueprinting for money or supply. Use orange for energy, yellow for wisdom and unfoldment, blue or violet for healing or spiritual attainment.

When you have chosen the color for the background of your blueprint, based on your primary need or desire, place at the top of the construction paper or whatever material you use a picture of Jesus, or a church, or a Bible, or some scene which is connected in your mind with God

. . . anything that signifies to you that God is the one and only Source of your good. Then paste your pictures on the paper or cardboard background. You will find a sample of one I made years ago on p. 58.

After you have constructed your blueprint, then expect it to work. Look at it as often as possible, especially before going to sleep at night; let your constant prayer be something like this:

THANK YOU, FATHER. I NOW ACCEPT THESE BLESSINGS OR SOMETHING BETTER, WITH GOOD TO ALL CONCERNED. MY GOOD COMES TO ME UNDER GRACE, IN PERFECT WAYS.

STEPS TO DEMONSTRATING YOUR PROSPERITY

- Make your Blueprint for Prosperity, listing:

    - One major goal (a new home, a trip, a better job).

    - One minor goal (a small appliance, new clothes).

    - One changed condition (greater happiness in the family . . . contentment on the job . . . more patience).

- Write out your list of daily, weekly and monthly goals to be achieved. Be realistic and practical, yet don't be too easy on yourself. Make lists that will keep you on your toes, mentally, physically and spiritually.

10

Be Enthusiastic

Again it was Emerson who gave us a clue to the accomplishment of goals when he said, "Nothing worthwhile is ever achieved without enthusiasm." Genuine enthusiasm is a definite mark of success . . . all successful people have it in some degree, and you must develop it if it is not now a part of your character. Find something about which you can really get excited . . . a football game, a contest, a new car, a trip . . . then practice that same kind of enthusiasm

in your prosperity program. Get really excited about the steps we are discussing. Remember, the word enthusiasm comes from the Greek words *en theos*, meaning "in God"; when you are enthusiastic, that very attitude is evidence of God's presence and activity in you.

11

Don't Give Up

Remember that you are replacing old, negative thoughts about yourself with fresh, new, positive ones, and this process does not always produce results instantaneously. It took you years to accumulate the ideas which have kept you limited and restricted. Now you are taking the steps to free yourself and live the abundant life promised by Jesus. Every journey begins with a single step and you have taken that first step by reading this book. The moment you start to fill your mind with these prosperous ideas, your transformation begins. In just reading these few pages you have changed your mind about money and your right to be prosperous. Make up your mind that you will not be side-tracked or delayed in your prosperity program because of laziness or discouragement.

A famous and very wealthy insurance tycoon attributes his success to these three little words: DO IT NOW.

Socrates was once asked the way to Mt. Olympus, and he answered, "Make every step you take go in that direction."

There is a whimsical little story about a snail and a cherry tree. The snail was inching its way up the trunk of the barren tree in the dead of winter, while some robins flew through the bare branches taunting the snail. "Where do you think you're going?" they teased. "To get some cherries," replied the snail. The robins laughed and called out, "Why you foolish thing! There *aren't* any cherries on this tree's branches." Patiently, the snail called back, "There will be when I get there."

12

Practice Praising God

In the Old Testament stories, we find that whenever the people got into trouble of any kind, they praised God. Moderns do not use spiritual power enough, and we find that when we do use it, it is regenerative.

In Paul's letter to the Thessalonians, he said this: "Always be joyful. Always keep on praying. No matter what happens, always be thankful, for this is God's will for you who belong to Christ Jesus." If you will begin to practice praising and thanking God for everything in your life, you'll soon find that you can't be low or depressed. As you turn to God in thanksgiving and praise, your spirits will begin to rise, and you will see opportunities and possibilities where none had seemed to exist before you began your expression of gratitude. If you think you need more money in order to be secure, your real need is to know God as your only source and supply.

A man told his minister that he had worked hard all his life, but somehow he never had enough to pay all the bills. Working overtime seemed to make little difference, and he lived with an increasing fear that some day he would not be able to keep up with the demands of his creditors. Someone told him about the power in praise,

71

and he saw that there was something wrong about the way he was trying to cope with his problem. He was determined to praise and thank God for every bill. That night when he sat down to write out the monthly checks, he looked at the largest and most urgent bill. He sat there, looking at the piece of paper for a moment, then said, "Thank you, Father, for this bill. Bless the check and the people who receive it." He felt so good about his first attempt at praising God that he continued, "Thank you, God, for this home and the mortgage on it. Thank you for heat and light and water. Thank you for my family and my good job. . . ." On and on he went.

As he wrote out check after check he found his spirits rising, and he went to bed that night with a light heart in spite of an empty bank account. Two days later he received an unexpected refund on his income tax; then someone he had owed wrote that the bill was in error and his debt was many dollars less than he had thought it to be. Within two weeks all his bills were paid in full, and he had as much money in the bank as he had had before he started to write his monthly checks. Coincidence? No, the inevitable consequence of praising and thanking God and trusting Him to handle things.

I heard of a woman who decided to praise her way through her difficulties, and on the day she started her praise and thanksgiving program, everything seemed to go wrong. Her child stayed home from school with a cold, the washing machine overflowed, the car wouldn't start and the dog ran away. When she sank down in a chair to thank God, she couldn't think of a single thing for which to be thankful, but she stated with resignation, "Thank you,

Lord. I don't know for what, but thank you anyway." She said it with feeling and she meant it. Within minutes she began to see the humor of the events of the day. She laughed aloud and later told a friend, "Nothing really happened, but I suddenly felt good, and knew that whatever happened the rest of the day, I could cope."

If you really want some miracles to happen try praising God for people who don't agree with you . . . people who may be a real trial in your life.

Several years ago I received in the mail a very abusive letter from a man who obviously had a hang-up about women ministers. He was brutally critical and unfair in his comments (he admitted that he had never met me). He did have the courage to sign his name, and my first human impulse was to write an equally scathing letter putting him in his place; but then I began to feel sorry for him. I thought of how unhappy he must be to have to resort to such abuses. Suddenly I thought, "I must thank God for that man and for this letter." So I prayed something like this: "Thank you, Father, that your grace is sufficient for me in this moment. You are supplying everything I need to handle this situation. Move into this man's life and fill that God-shaped vacuum with your love and forgiveness and acceptance. Thank you."

After that I dictated a letter to the disgruntled man, thanking him for his interest and sending blessings and good wishes, entirely ignoring the hostile tone of his letter to me.

It was a day of real healing for me, and for him, too, I trust.

Sometimes, when we are so intent on learning the new mental and spiritual attitudes which are stepping stones to our new prosperity, we forget to practice the art of appreciation. All forms of life respond to appreciation, expressed and demonstrated. Begin today to give thanks for the half-full cup instead of the half-empty one. Take time to tell your family members and your business associates how much you appreciate them. You know how children, animals and even flowers and plants respond to warmth, love and praise. All life responds in one way or another. Harshness, criticism and lack of appreciation tend to shrivel and stifle all forms of life, from people to plants, while praise, love and appreciation evoke the same emotions and actions from people who are the recipients of such attention. Don't forget to say "Thank you" at the slightest provocation. Those two words are magic: they can melt the hardest heart and bring out the best in anyone.

STEPS TO PRAISE-FUL LIVING:

- Find at least five things each day for which to praise God. Remember that we are to praise Him for ALL things, not just the pleasant experiences in our lives. Discover for yourself the magical change which takes place when you form the habit of praising Him in all things.

- Say "Thank you" to at least five people each day (Try to find unusual reasons for expressing your appreciation).

13

Tithe Your Way to Total Prosperity

The most important lesson in the whole Bible is one which God demonstrated on three of the six days of creation. This principle is repeated six times in Genesis alone and over again and again in the rest of the Bible. EVERYTHING REPRODUCES AFTER ITS KIND.

You may remember the story of Elijah and the widow. When the widow needed food and money to pay her bills, Elijah didn't turn the stones in her garden into bread, nor bring gold out of thin air. Instead he asked, "What do you have in the house?" He showed her that she must start with what she had. As she followed Elijah's directions and began to pour out the tiny bit of oil, it continued to multiply and kept flowing until every container she had or could borrow was full. Only then did the oil stop flowing.

There are many schemes and gimmicks which promise a person instant riches, but most of them fail. There is one infallible formula for abundance which has never yet been known to fail the person who uses it. It has been used for thousands of years by people of all religions and races and cultures. It is based upon spiritual principles that are as dependable as the law of gravity. The infallible formula is simply this: Take God into partnership and agree to give Him 10% of all income, expected and unexpected.

It is amazing that more people don't know about this idea and that those who do know of it are often reluctant to try it. Some people think it is too simple. The principle behind its effectiveness is this: there is just one basic substance, God, who is both the substance itself and the Source of that substance. This one substance comes into visibility in an infinite number of forms, including money, energy and health.

This basic substance, regardless of the form it takes, has to flow through a channel. It must have an outlet as well as an intake.

This substance can only flow into human experience when an outlet, or channel, has been provided for it; this substance is inseparably one with all other forms of good. So what is good for one must be good for all.

Your lungs must be emptied before you can take another breath. If you want light in your home, you must turn the switch so that power can flow through the electrical wires.

To have abundance in your experience, you must give before you receive. If you have little, you still must begin to give of whatever you have, if you would have an increase. Jesus understood this law of giving and receiving when He said, "Give and it shall be given unto you."

Giving 10% to God's work is called *tithing*.

Originally a tithe was a percentage of flocks, herds and produce. This percentage given to God's work was always the best of the lot. After the advent of money as a medium of exchange, the practice was continued, with the individual giving at least one-tenth of all monies received to some channel of religious work. It must be remembered that a tithe is neither a gift, a reward, an act of charity nor payment for services. It is one-tenth or more of one's income, LEFT with the Source of all things as belonging to that Source. It is left that you may never sever your contact with the Source.

The successful farmer follows the plan of tithing perfectly and scientifically where his crops are concerned. One-tenth of his best seed is kept for replanting and is returned to the soil to perpetuate the process of growth. Again, the sown seed is not a gift, nor compensation. It belongs to the soil as an inseparable part of nature's plan to supply the needs of all forms of creation. Not only is the best seed saved and planted, but the ground is prepared and supported in the best possible manner (attitudes of receptivity, praise, blessing).

The actual purpose of tithing is found in the book of Malachi in the Old Testament. *Bring ye all the tithes into the storehouse, that there may be meat in my house, and prove me now herewith, saith the Lord of hosts, if I will not open the windows of heaven, and pour you out such a blessing, that there shall not be room enough to receive it.* Malachi 3:10

It is evident from this statement that the first motive of one who tithes should be the support of that individual or organization engaged in spiritual activity, where the knowledge and power of God is promoted. The tithe is definitely for the support of spiritual ministries that extend and expand the work of the Creator.

Tithing is a part of the law of sowing and reaping. Where there is definite contact preserved between cause and effect, the effect is supported and perpetuated. If a break in the connection occurs, the effect must diminish accordingly.

Have you wondered why your prayers for prosperity haven't worked? Now you know the most likely reason for their failure—there was a break in the contact. When the prodigal son separated his inheritance from the father, it soon dissipated itself. Tithing preserves your contact. It keeps your affairs in touch with the creative power of the universe.

Are you old enough to remember having seen your grandmother churn butter? You know that the milk is allowed to stand in a cool place until the cream rises to the top; then it is scooped off and churned until it becomes rich butter. Why does God ask us to give off the top? Because that's where the cream is, and what you give He multiplies back to you. Do you want to give Him the skimmed milk and have Him multiply that? Remember, everything reproduces after its kind, so give the best that you have and the best will come back to you.

And tithe your time, not just your money! How many minutes a day do you give to God's work through prayer for your loved ones and the world, as well as yourself?

A sales manager whose success was the talk of his industry, attributed his effectiveness to the fact that before every hour of selling or speaking to his sales force, he spent 6 minutes (a tenth of an hour) in prayer and meditation.

Have you ever tried to tithe your love, your goodwill? I think you'll find that you can't limit yourself to 10%.

A man who tithed regularly still did not prosper and he was puzzled. One day, in meditation, he discovered that he had not completely released his tithe. It was always given accompanied by a nagging feeling deep within him that he was depleting his own supply. When he discovered the error in his attitude and came to understand that one can never outgive God, prosperity began to flow into his life.

Another man said, "I tithe, but I still can't make my bills each month. What's wrong?" In conversation with a friend, he found that the culprit was his attitude: "I don't want anything back, I don't expect anything."

The Bible says that a man shall decree a thing and it shall be established unto him . . . it will come to pass. This man had given the order to his subconscious mind and it had implicitly obeyed him. He changed his attitude and his expectancy, and used this affirmation many times a day:

I GIVE IN JOY AND FREEDOM AND RECEIVE WITH GRATITUDE AND PRAISE.

You see, we are working with an infallible law and such a law always works, not just sometimes, ALWAYS!

When you get into the practice of tithing, you will be impressed with what a great idea it is. It's so fair. If you don't earn a dollar, God doesn't expect anything. If you earn a dollar He expects only a dime. If you earn $1,000, He expects $100. If you earn $20,000, He expects $2,000. You pay the bank 10% to borrow money and you expect to pay it back. God only asks 10% and you can keep the rest. God is a better manager than man. His 10% goes so much further than our 90%. That may be another reason why tithers prosper. They are forced to re-examine their outgo. Nearly every person who has a financial problem does not suffer from a lack of income. It's usually a problem of outgo, an unwise handling of the available supply. When you make the commitment to tithe, God will automatically give you the wisdom to manage your money in a better way. Bargains will come your way . . . you will find unexpected values . . . you will be spared expenses which you have previously had.

This is a giving universe. "Give and it shall be given unto you." The law works whether you want it to or not. Where there is no voluntary giving, something is taken away. Often people who think they can not afford to tithe have to give anyway . . . they are overcharged for services . . . they seem prone to accidents and business problems. If you don't give voluntarily of your financial resources, you can expect confusion and problems of all kinds. You can only cheat yourself out of much health, wealth and happiness by foolishly trying to avoid the law of giving.

A tithe without love and a feeling of freedom and expansiveness is mockery. With love, your giving is a spiritual service and an act of worship.

He that soweth sparingly shall reap sparingly; and he that soweth bountifully shall also reap bountifully. Let each man give according as he hath purposed in his heart, not grudgingly or of necessity, for God loveth a cheerful giver. 2nd Corinthians 9:6,7

The basis of tithing is recognition of God's ownership and man's stewardship. It is completely in harmony with the laws of nature. The law of prosperity is governed by harmony just as are the seasons, the tides, the rhythm of music, the orderly movement of stars and planets. When you tithe you get in tune with the basic order and harmony of the universe. You feel more at one with all people and all nature, and there is a deep feeling of belonging to the whole.

One of the most exciting and rewarding adventures in giving is experienced when one gives right after a loss of some kind. Such giving demonstrates real faith, and it is always honored by God. A woman whose home was destroyed by fire was taken in by some neighbors; on the morning after the fire, as she sat looking at the few belongings she had managed to salvage, she got out her checkbook and wrote out a check to her church. Then she asked her kind hostess if she could have a stamp with which to mail her check to the church that very morning. Her neighbor cried out, "You mean you are giving something to the church after what you've lost? The church should be giving something to *you* after all the years you have contributed and helped in so many ways!" The homeless woman replied, "Oh, I know the church doesn't need this money. I know too that I have many places for every dime, but I need to give. I need to feel my contact with God and to prove to myself my faith that God will continue to supply all my needs."

Before her letter was in the mailbox, there was a telephone call from a friend, telling her of someone who was looking for a house-sitter for six months. The contact was made and arrangements completed. The owner of the house was a wealthy widower; when he returned from his six months' cruise, he was so delighted with the condition of his lovely home, noting the obvious love and care which had been lavished upon it by his house-sitter, that he asked her to stay on permanently. The story has a beautiful ending because these two were eventually married. To this day the happy wife declares that her good was on its way to her the moment she decided to prove her faith by making her contribution to her church. She knows that had she spent her time moaning and fretting over her losses, God would never have been able to work so speedily and beautifully to bring even greater good into her life. Her generosity and thankfulness for life made her an open channel for God's lavish abundance to pour into her life.

The Psalmist said: "I have been young and now am old, but I have never seen the righteous forsaken nor his seed begging bread. The law of God is in his heart and none of his steps shall slide."

Many of the stories I would like to share with you seem like miracles. A miracle is not something supernatural or mysterious. It is something which is a result of the working of a law or principle we do not yet understand. In demonstrating prosperity, a miracle is not something you get for nothing. Miracles take place when you give first, proving your faith and trust in the One Source. The wisest man of all time said, "Cast your bread upon the waters, for you shall find it after many days." Your bread, of course, includes your money, your time, your energy, your talents, your faith and your love. When you cast your bread, when you give, your good may return on another wave. That is, your good may not necessarily return through the person or organization to which you gave, but that is not your concern. Your job, and mine, is to give, knowing that through the working of immutable law, the return is inevitable: it cannot be avoided.

When the soul begins to fuse with the Father, you will want to give. You cannot help it. When the contact is made, you become one with the Father and take on the givingness of God's nature.

Perhaps a personal experience will help you to understand just how exacting and dependable is this law of giving and receiving. Several years ago my husband retired from a large symphony orchestra after 30 years of a happy and rewarding career as a musician. His decision to retire was prompted not by age, but because of some extensive dental work which needed to be done. As he was writing his letter of resignation, he was offered a full professorship at a large western university for the following year. During the time of his temporary disability, before the medical compensations and salary adjustments could be made, he received no salary. However, I continued to write out the weekly check to the church just as if he had received his usual paycheck. (We had tithed for many years on our combined income and continued this practice even when only my salary was coming in.) Many months later, when the insurance money and back-salary came, the total amount was ten times the amount we had given to the church!

At an earlier time in our lives, at the very beginning of our tithing adventure, I decided that God could wait one month. There were so many extra bills that month, so I withheld the tithe and didn't say anything about it to my husband. When he went to our accountant to take care of our income tax, he called me from the tax man's office. His voice was a bit chilly and I knew he had found me out! He asked, "Did you withhold anything from our tithing money last year?" I had to reply, weakly, "Yes, 300 dollars." There was a moment's silence and he said, "I knew it. Our income went down by $3,000 last year."

The more you give or use, the more you will receive and have.

It has been said, and I have proved the validity of these statements, that the person who begins to tithe will have at least six surprises. He will be surprised . . .

at the amount of money he has for God's work

at the deepening of his spiritual life

at the ease with which he can meet his personal obligation

at the joy with which he can go from 10% to larger giving

at the preparation tithing gives him for being a faithful and wise steward of the remaining 90%

and

at himself, for not adopting the plan sooner.

14

Some Questions and Answers on Tithing

Q. But I barely have enough money to go around now! How can I give any, let alone 10%, to God?

A. If that is your feeling about your condition, then you can't afford *not* to tithe. A businessman, after attending a prosperity class in his church, informed his accountant the next morning that he had decided to tithe 10% of his gross income. His accountant protested, "Man, you must be crazy! You'll be broke in six months!" But six months later the business was more prosperous than ever, and one day the minister who had presented the prosperity class had a call from the skeptical accountant. The man had been so impressed with the increased success of the business and his boss's obvious new prosperity that he wanted to know all about it for himself!

Q. Where do I give the tithe? To a person or an organization?

A. You give your tithe money to that person or organization through which your good comes to you—the church where you are spiritually fed, or the spiritual group to which you belong and which you honestly feel is doing a faithful job of promoting God's work. You may give to a person who has been a source of spiritual strength to you. For tax deduction, the government recognizes only those donations made to authorized charitable organizations, such as churches or philanthropic movements. But make sure your gift is to a God-centered channel which is teaching the truth and doing something to help others.

Q. I belong to a church in another city where we used to live. I feel that I must be loyal to that church, but I am attending a church near my new home and am getting so much good out of its teachings, I don't know where to give my tithe money.

A. You wouldn't have a meal in one restaurant, then go down the street and pay the bill in another restaurant. The tithe is to be paid to that channel through which your spiritual sustenance comes to you. Further, God speaks and acts by means of man (you and me) as channels. You look to an individual or organization as a channel through which you receive spiritual help. In turn, it is perfectly within the province of spiritual practice that you should be the channel through which God supplies the church or ministry. To safeguard your own best interests, you should help to make your chosen channel of spiritual refreshment as strong as possible. You should strive in thought, word and deed to perfect it; as you do, you lift the standards of your community, and therefore improve your own environment. A starved spiritual ministry cannot give to you or the members of your community the best spiritual support. See that there is "meat in my house" and God's work will be in the best possible position to serve you and those around you.

Q. How is the tithe paid—weekly, monthly, or yearly?

A. The tithe is ideally paid as soon as you get your paycheck or investment check or dividend . . . in whatever form your supply comes to you. We have found that it is good to make out the tithe check before paying other bills. Somehow, the remaining 90% seems to go farther than the 100% ever did!

Q. God doesn't need my money as much as I do. Shouldn't my own obligations come first?

A. Of course God doesn't need your money! But He does need your trust and your confidence in Him, and you do need to learn that He is the only Source of all good. Prayer doesn't change God; it simply puts us in tune with His perfect will, so that that will can be done in and through us. Tithing establishes divine order in our lives. It is evidence of our belief in God's work and of our desire to support and sustain that work. It makes us partners with God in the greatest enterprise on earth—the bringing forth of His kingdom on earth.

Q. What about giving to the poor and to needy relatives?

A. Many people think this is a justifiable form of tithing, but it is not. The tithe is always given to that channel through which one's own good is received, such as a church, or healing group, or practitioner. Giving unwisely to relatives or friends often robs them of their own incentive and initiative. When people receive help too easily and too frequently, they often become dependent and ultimately cease to be motivated to do anything for themselves. The finest and most lasting gift you can give another is the knowledge of the laws of prosperity.

Q. I've made some foolish investments. Do you think God wants to help me get out of the muddle of my mixed up affairs?

A. God does want you to prosper, but He will not "reward" you for your lack of wisdom or vision. This may seem to contradict the Bible verse that "With God all things are possible," but it doesn't. God is wisdom and intelligence, and by allowing God to guide and direct your decisions and actions, He will help you to redeem your mistakes. You will find that if you truly trust Him and make every effort to follow His directions, you will realize greater abundance than you would ever have reaped from your foolish investment, had it worked out for you.

Q. I am deeply in debt. I hate this condition and would give anything to be free of all debts. What can I do?

A. Don't dwell on the ideal of being free from debt, because debts are an evidence of spiritual advancement; but you should not be burdened with debts. There is a great difference between simply having a debt and being burdened with anxiety and fear about debts. You will never rid yourself of debt as long as you fear and dread it. When you think of debt as an evil thing, you are giving it power over you. In fact, you are binding it to you. Understand what debt really is: it means credit. No debt can exist without a credit. A debt means that someone trusted you. Change your attitude about debts. Stop thinking of them as something to avoid. Think of debt as a symbol of trust, of the faith that others have in you. Bless those to whom you owe money. Be honest and sincere in wanting to pay your just debts. Know that you have the infinite God with you in your desire and efforts to pay your debts. Know that as long as you can create, you have the means whereby you can pay your debt. God Himself cannot work through a worried mind. As long as you give more attention to your indebtedness than you give to the power of God to create through you, you are not giving God a chance to help you. God is able to meet all the debts in the world. He is eager to work through you to move you into a state of fluidity and flow, as money comes to you, goes out from you, and comes again into your experience, all in a beautiful, natural rhythm.

Tithing is the one sure way to experience lasting, dependable, over-flowing abundance in your life. It is the one practice which makes the whole prosperity principle work so effectively.

- Tithing increases your faith in God and in yourself.

- It helps you to see that your failures and setbacks are temporary.

- It establishes order and harmony.

- It gives you absolute confidence that you are tied in with the only Source and the only Supply in the universe.

- Its spiritual reward is greater than any blessing of which you can conceive.

- It helps you to understand that God never puts anything in a closed hand.

Someday you are going to have an exciting story to share, a story of the journey from lack to limitless, abundant living; but God isn't going to give you the chance to tell such a story until you first give yourself a chance and begin to manage your money God's way.

God doesn't even ask you to take His promises on faith. Just give Him the first tenth and you can feel secure, knowing that you and God have made a contract. You need never again worry or be anxious. You are going to prosper in the worst times. Try it! And know that . . .

GOD IS BLESSING YOU NOW—ALWAYS AND IN ALL WAYS!

15

It Works!

As final proof that the ideas in this book will work for you, let me share some letters from newly prospered people:

As a result of your Prosperity Class and because of the new insights which have come to us, we have decided to go into a new venture which has been "teasing" us for some time. We have been afraid to take the step until now. It is interesting to see that the fear is directly related to seeing ourselves as the "source" of our own prosperity. To recognize the Universal Source is to be free of the heavy responsibility that follows trying to manage your life all by yourself.

D. M.
Newport Beach, Calif.

After just two days of using the prosperity principles presented in your class, things began to happen. My husband got an unexpected raise, and my kids came home with the best report cards they have ever had. That is prosperity, isn't it? Also, I ended the month with $40 left over in my grocery money. Usually the amount I set aside for food never goes far enough. Something is happening and I can hardly wait to see what comes next!

Mrs. A. M.
Newport Beach, Calif.

The most wonderful thing has happened to me. I started tithing to my church the day after you gave the class and I wrote lists of things for which I am thankful, things I want to come into my life, and people that I forgive and want to forgive me. Like a bolt out of the blue, I got a call from TWA (I used to work for them and have wanted to again). They were calling to offer me a job at a much higher salary than I am making, and here's the clincher. They want me to begin work a week from now, and in San Francisco, where my family lives!

C. C.
Honolulu

Both my friend and I felt so "light" after the class . . . we simply had shed all negatives.

G. B.
Honolulu

The thing that really impresses me most about this new concept of prosperity is that I know for the first time that I am a child of God. He is my Father and He wants me to have all the abundance of the earth. My earthly parents were always so bad off that I had to help them through the worst years. I am thankful that I could help, but it's so nice to know that I have a new "Dad," who can do what He says He will do. I feel like a happy kid again.

B. K.
Arcadia, Calif.

I have made the decision to tithe and it feels so good. I feel wealthy, prosperous and secure. God doesn't have a bigger shovel. He has a DUMP TRUCK!

C. W.
Arcadia, Calif.

Just wanted to let you know that our business (God's and mine) is doing fantastic! Taking God into partnership is the wisest move I ever made.

D. M.
Arcadia, Calif.

My need is not for money. I met that need in the last prosperity class and money will never again be a problem. My need is for more time. Through this study I realized that I don't need more time, but wiser use of the time I have. New ways have begun to open up for me to put down a false sense of responsibility and give me freedom to be myself. As a result, I am beginning to feel a bubbling up from within of joy and well-being—a fulfillment I have never experienced before.

E. G.
San Gabriel, Calif.

The favorite hobby of the entire family is flying.

Margaret M. Stevens has been minister of the beautiful and prosperous Santa Anita Church for the past 20 years. She is also Director of the Barnhart School, a fully accredited Christian day school for children, kindergarten through eighth grade, and Founder-Director of the Santa Anita Center for Ministerial Studies. For the past eighteen years she has traveled throughout the world (five times to South Africa) to present her sparkling, practical prosperity classes. This book is the essence of her demonstrable, down-to-earth approach to the subject of supply.

In private life, Margaret Stevens is the wife of Roger S. Stevens, for 30 years a member of the Los Angeles Philharmonic Orchestra, now Professor of Music at the University of Southern California.

The family includes two sons, a daughter and four grandchildren. Their son David, a commercial artist, is illustrator for his mother in this book as well as in her first three books, the *Stepping Stones* books for children.

In honor of her 20th anniversary as minister of the Arcadia Church, a beautiful new educational building was added to the Santa Anita campus, and named MARGARET STEVENS CENTER.